STEVE JOBS

SARA ABRAHAM
CO-AUTHOR

REDA JABER
CO-AUTHOR

JOAQUIN ARIAS
ILLUSTRATOR

www.visionary-kids.com

It was a wintery day in the City of San Francisco, when a surprise emerged through a foggy window.

On that day a precious baby was born.
But his parents were sad, their hearts were torn.

With tears in her eyes the mother did weep,
for he was a baby that she could not keep.

The day came where she had to say goodbye.
She dressed him in blue, he matched the sky.

His adoptive mother said, "I shall name him Steven Paul" Then Mrs. Jobs carefully wrapped Steve in a soft, knitted shawl.

The Jobs family welcomed Steve with open arms.
He would be their pride and joy, their new little charm.

Steve Jobs grew up fast and boy, was he bright.
He built contraptions that would send things in flight.

When Steve turned five, his family moved to a new town.
It was not far – only an hour drive down.

During elementary school he would often daydream.
Huddled over his papers, he planned ways to scheme.

Between classes, Steve carried out his pranks.
These were sure to earn him quite a few spanks!

At home, Steve played with toys so much they'd break.
But he always tried to fix them, no matter how long it'd take.

One day at school he proclaimed, "This is a bore."
So he up packed and left – he sought to explore!

Steve loved to work with gadgets and art.
So he gathered some friends – this was the start.

The group used Steve's garage as a place to invent.
They worked all day and all night until they felt spent.

They continued to tinker, they continued to create.
They knew, sooner or later, they would have something great!

Finally one day they created something really cool:
A computer that worked as a personal tool!

They founded the company and called it Apple.
It was a name that was easy to grapple.

Steve Jobs used his imagination with each new creation.
People around the world thought he was a true inspiration.

Steve and his team helped create many new things, that all kinds of people could use, from kids to kings.

Always ask questions, always seek to explore.
And make sure to take risks, else life is a bore.

Pursue your dreams and don't let stumbles make you blue.
For when you're on top, there can be no better view.

THANK YOU KICKSTARTER BACKERS

Funded! This project was successfully funded on March 27.

"Life can be much broader once you discover one simple fact...and that is everything around you that you call life was made up by people no smarter than you and you can change it. You can influence it. You can build your own things that other people can use. Once you learn that, you'll never be the same person again!"

"I'm convinced that about half of what separates the successful entrepreneurs from the non-successful ones is pure perseverance."

"Innovation distinguishes between a leader and a follower."

"Creativity is just connecting things. When you ask creative people how they did something, they feel a little guilty because they didn't really do it, they just saw something. It seemed obvious to them after a while."

"Quality is more important than quantity. One home run is much better than two doubles."

"Here's to the crazy ones, the misfits, the rebels, the troublemakers, the round pegs in the square holes... The ones who see things differently — they're not fond of rules... You can quote them, disagree with them, glorify or vilify them, but the only thing you can't do is ignore them because they change things... They push the human race forward, and while some may see them as the crazy ones, we see genius, because the ones who are crazy enough to think that they can change the world, are the ones who do."

Make This Your Personal Audio Book!

StorySticker™
all you read is love

FLHJPSWMLF

To get started:
1. Download the free StorySticker app, or visit www.storysticker.com
2. Set up an account
3. Scan or enter the code above
4. Record yourself reading the story one page at a time and save when finished

Visionary Kids: Steve Jobs
Copyright © 2014 by Sara Abraham and Reda Jaber
Original Illustrations by Joaquin Arias
Printed by CreateSpace
ISBN: 978-0-9960848-0-2
URL: http://www.visionary-kids.com

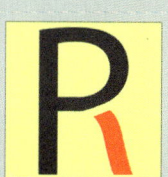 Rocky's Pillow Publishing, LLC
info@rockyspillow.com
http://www.rockyspillow.com

All rights reserved. No part of this publication may be reproduced, stored in a retrieval system, or transmitted, in any form or by any means, electronic, mechanical, photocopying, recording, or otherwise, without prior written permission of the authors.